21st Century Skills Library

COOL CAREERS

VETERINARIAN

Barbara A. Somervill

Cherry Lake Publishing
Ann Arbor, Michigan

Published in the United States of America by Cherry Lake Publishing
Ann Arbor, Michigan
www.cherrylakepublishing.com

Content Adviser: David Vail, Diplomate ACVIM (Oncology) and Professor of Oncology, School of Veterinary Medicine, University of Wisconsin–Madison.

Photo Credits: Cover and page 1, ©iStockphoto.com/thecarsonimage; page 4, ©Victor Watts/Alamy; page 6, ©iStockphoto.com/photomorphic; page 8, ©iStockphoto.com/ dem10; page 11, ©iStockphoto.com/elrphoto; page 12, ©Mark William Penny, used under license from Shutterstock, Inc.; page 14, ©Wendy Kaveney Photography, used under license from Shutterstock, Inc.; page 15, ©iStockphoto.com/hayesphotography; page 17, ©Enigma/Alamy; page 18, ©iStockphoto.com/mrloz; page 20, ©The Photolibrary Wales/Alamy; page 23, ©Corbis Premium RF/Alamy; page 24, ©ian cruickshank/Alamy; page 27, ©iStockphoto.com/Nnehring

Library of Congress Cataloging-in-Publication Data
Somervill, Barbara A.
Veterinarian / by Barbara A. Somervill.
    p. cm.—(Cool careers)
Includes index.
ISBN-13: 978-1-60279-301-9
ISBN-10: 1-60279-301-8
1. Veterinarians—Juvenile literature. 2. Veterinary medicine—Vocational guidance—Juvenile literature. I. Title. II. Series.
SF756.S66 2009
636.089'023—dc22   2008014094

Cherry Lake Publishing would like to acknowledge the work of The Partnership for 21st Century Skills.

Please visit www.21stcenturyskills.org for more information.

TABLE OF CONTENTS

CHAPTER ONE

THE HISTORY OF VETERINARY MEDICINE

Teamwork is often required when veterinarians work with large animals.

The veterinary team located the injured bull elephant along the shore of Lake Vembo. They quickly shot the elephant with a tranquilizer dart. Heavily sedated, the elephant sat down. It would now be safe to examine and treat the animal's wound. Exotic animal vets Sharon Deem and Stephen Black removed the snare from the elephant's leg. The wound was very deep. The vets hoped the elephant would recover full use of its leg. They treated the wound and gave the elephant penicillin and a tetanus shot.

A few days later, the bull elephant was spotted feeding in the area. He was moving well and appeared to be on his way to a full recovery. For the two vets, it was just another day on the job. Both vets are trained in healing exotic animals and wildlife. Veterinarians work to make sure that animals everywhere are being taken care of.

About 10,000 years ago, humans in Mesopotamia began domesticating animals. Mesopotamia is an area between the Tigris and Euphrates rivers in southwest Asia. They raised goats, cattle, pigs, and sheep on their farms. Goats

Herders depend on animals to make a living. Veterinarians work hard to keep the herds healthy.

and sheep provided hair and wool for making cloth. Goats and cattle provided milk for cheese and butter. Animals were also slaughtered to provide meat. Raising these animals meant having the responsibility of caring for them. For thousands of years, that duty fell on farmers and herders.

Healers who took care of humans also delivered foals, calves, and lambs. They were called on to treat sick and wounded animals. Records of these early veterinary efforts appear in an Egyptian medical textbook that is almost 4,000 years old. The text describes diseases of cattle, dogs, and birds. Other Egyptian texts show an understanding of animal anatomy, symptoms of animal diseases, and specific treatments. The Romans, Greeks, and Hebrews also had healers who cared for animals.

By the 1700s, people in Europe and North America felt the need for doctors who could take care of their animals. Farmers had to keep their livestock healthy. They depended on horses or mules for transportation. They sold cattle, sheep, or pigs to make money. They also wanted to prevent diseased animals from spreading the illness to humans. These needs led to the establishment of veterinary schools.

The first veterinarians did not have the tools, such as x-rays machines, that are available today.

The first veterinary school in Europe was founded in Lyons, France, in 1761. The Royal Veterinary School provided courses in the anatomy and diseases of horses, cattle, and sheep. Vets at the time worked mostly with farm animals. They did not often take care of dogs or cats as they do today.

Most farm animal diseases did not spread until steamships and airplanes became popular transportation. Many contagious animals were brought over to North America. Farmers and doctors were afraid that these animals would spread unwanted diseases. As a result, the Ontario Veterinary College of the University of Guelph (in Canada) started in 1862. It is the oldest veterinary school currently open in North America. The School of Veterinary Medicine of the University of Pennsylvania is the oldest veterinary college in the United States.

Advances in veterinary medicine came along with advances in human medicine. It is hard to believe, but 85 years ago, there were no antibiotics for humans or animals. Today, we have new medicines that prevent problems such as heartworm, fleas, and ticks.

Surgical instruments and techniques have improved, too. The use of X-rays to diagnose broken bones benefits animals as well as humans. Anesthesia for animals has also improved, making it safer to operate on animals. A modern vet's office has much of the same equipment as a modern doctor's office.

CHAPTER TWO

A Day in the Life of a Vet

*Veterinarians who work with large animals are often
called in to help mares deliver healthy foals.*

The day begins quite early for this veterinarian, who
works on both small and large animals. Being called in
the middle of the night is not too unusual. Tonight, the
call is from a horse farm. One of the mares is in labor and
having a difficult time delivering her foal. The vet arrives at

Helping an animal during the birthing process can be stressful.
Vets must be able to stay calm and think quickly.

2:30 AM It is dark and cold, and the vet is tired, but those things do not matter. What's important is the health of the mare and her baby. The delivery takes a little more than three hours. It's a girl!

After the delivery, there is time for a quick shower and breakfast before heading to the office. This morning, the vet has a full appointment book. The first three patients are having surgery. The first one is being spayed—an operation that prevents female animals from having babies. Then a male cat is having a tumor removed. Finally, a frisky dog needs anesthesia to have a broken tooth pulled. Vets are not just animal doctors—they can also be animal dentists.

Later, a beagle puppy comes in for its shots. Vets give animals vaccines to prevent diseases. These shots are like the ones that human children get from their doctors.

As the morning wears on, the vet examines and treats dogs and cats of all ages. It is always a good idea to have

British vet James Alfred Wight, better known as James Herriot, wrote many books about his experience as a vet in England's Yorkshire Dales. Here is what Wight said about being a vet:

"I hope to make people realize how totally helpless animals are, how dependent on us, trusting as a child must that we will be kind and take care of their needs . . . [They] are an obligation put on us, a responsibility we have no right to neglect, nor to violate by cruelty."

Today, more than ever, many people are taking responsibility for protecting all of Earth's living things. They work together to help keep animals safe and healthy.

A veterinarian checks a dog's eyes during a checkup.

a new puppy or kitten checked over by a vet, to make sure it is healthy. The vet even sees a parrot with a broken beak.

Some animal patients have conditions that need medicine. Just after lunch, a large dog comes in with a serious tear in its skin. The dog cut its leg as it went over a fence. The wound must be examined carefully and cleaned. To make sure that the dog feels no pain, the vet gives it a shot of anesthetic. The

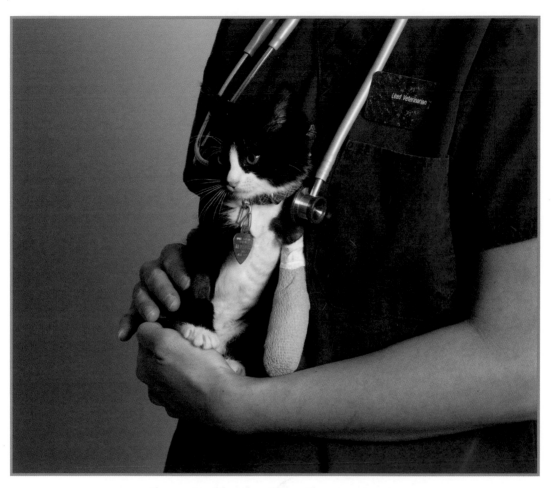

If an animal breaks a bone, the vet may put a cast on the injured area to help it heal.

wound is stitched and bandaged. With a little time to heal, the dog will be just fine.

During some free time, the vet visits the surgery patients from earlier in the day. The vet takes their temperatures and listens to their breathing. They are all doing fine.

Blood test results for three of yesterday's patients have arrived from the lab. The vet reviews the reports and calls the pet owners with the results. Vets also prescribe medicines for their patients. Owners can usually pick up the medication from the vet's office.

Late in the day, a call comes in from the local humane society. A dog that was struck by a car has been found on the highway. The vet and his assistants clear out a surgical room. A van arrives with the wounded dog in the back. The vet X-rays the wounded dog's leg. It is broken, and the bone will need to be set. The dog is given an anesthetic. The dog's leg is set, and the vet's day comes to an end.

It is 6:30 PM The vet does a quick check of the animals that will remain in care overnight. After that,

Veterinarians give animals medicine to make
them sleep before performing surgery.

the vet leaves for the day. It has been a long day, but very rewarding. The vet has used his experience and training to help many animals.

CHAPTER THREE

EDUCATION AND TRAINING

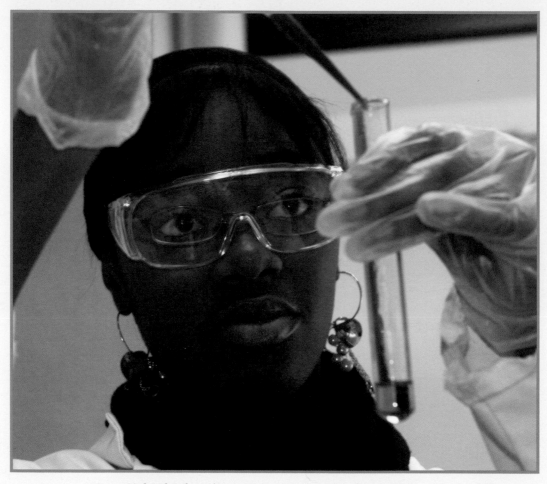

High school students can start preparing for veterinary school by taking as many science classes as possible.

Becoming a vet may be harder than becoming a medical doctor or a dentist. Fewer veterinary colleges exist than medical schools. Many people compete for the spots that are open. Only the top students are accepted, and those students come from all over the world.

Potential vets must first earn an undergraduate degree at a college or university. They should study mathematics, chemistry, biology, and physical science. As an undergraduate, a background in these subjects is particularly helpful. Students who want to apply to vet school take the Veterinary Aptitude Test (VAT), Medical College Admission Test (MCAT), or the Graduate Record Examination (GRE). These tests are usually given to college students before they graduate. Acceptance into vet school depends on a student's grades, activities, and his or her results on one of these tests.

The American Veterinary Medical Association certifies 28 colleges and schools of veterinary medicine in the United States. These schools meet the standards for quality

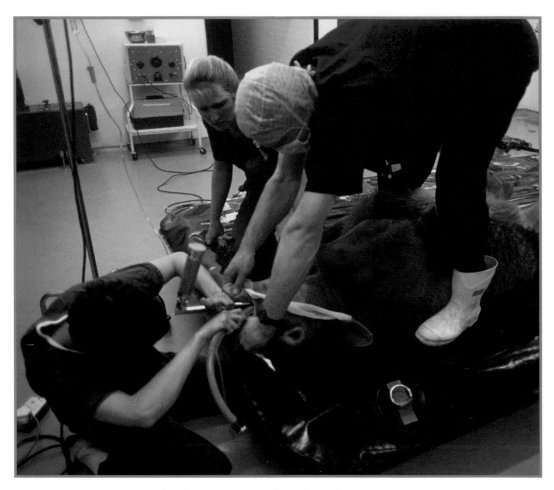

Veterinary school students learn how to use a variety of tools to perform surgery.

veterinary learning. Veterinarians must be licensed in the state where they work.

Students in veterinary school follow a four-year course of study. They learn how to treat a variety of animals. In the first two years, students learn the basics about animal anatomy. They also learn about various diseases, how to diagnose diseases, and about available treatments and medicines. Students spend most of their time in classrooms and laboratories during the first two years of veterinary school.

A student's last two years include more hands-on experience with animals. Students treat animals and perform surgery under the supervision of licensed veterinarians. This helps students gain valuable experience. At graduation, students will have spent about 4,000 hours in the classroom, laboratory, and doing clinical studies. Each year, slightly more than 2,000 new vets receive Doctor of Veterinary Medicine (DVM) degrees in the United States.

Veterinary education doesn't stop after graduation. Licensed vets often attend classes, workshops, and

Learning & Innovation Skills

Are you interested in becoming a veterinarian? You can learn how to handle animals through a variety of community programs. The 4-H organization throughout North America teaches members how to raise, care for, and breed a variety of animals. You can also volunteer at local animal shelters, animal health clinics, and zoos.

Why do you think people volunteer to take care of animals? What can people learn from these kinds of volunteer activities?

seminars. They must learn about new techniques for treating diseases. They also need to keep up with advances in equipment and medicine. Getting a degree and a license is not the end of learning—it is only the beginning.

CHAPTER FOUR

A Future with Animals

Dogs are one of the most common animals seen in veterinarians' offices.

Today, most vets treat small household pets, such as dogs, cats, lizards, and birds. This is called small animal practice. Some vets treat larger animals, such as horses, cattle, goats,

Some animals, such as pandas, are in danger of becoming extinct. Zoo veterinarians help them reproduce and stay healthy.

and sheep. Those vets usually live in rural areas where farmers need help caring for their animals.

There are many other areas of veterinary medicine in which vets can practice. Some vets treat exotic animals. They work in zoos, aquariums, and nature preserves and for government agencies. A zoo vet must know how to treat animals of all different sizes. Zoo vets work in zoos, wild animal parks, and circuses. Zoo vets can also be wildlife vets and work in wilderness areas. Marine vets take care of sea creatures. Marine vets usually work in aquariums.

About 2,000 vets work for the federal government in the Departments of Agriculture, Defense, and Health Services. They inspect meat and poultry and help prevent the spread of disease through animals.

Vets may also do research on animal and human diseases and the effects of various chemicals on animals, people, and the environment. They may work with

The Humane Society works to ensure that all types of animals are treated kindly. The society runs dog and cat shelters. It also arranges for wounded wild animals to be treated. The Humane Society University is a program designed for people interested in animal protection. The school is run jointly with Duquesne University. Students can earn a bachelor of science degree in humane leadership or a master's degree in community leadership. These programs help people develop strong leadership skills. Many people who graduate from these programs go on to work for nonprofit organizations that benefit animals.

Do you think humane treatment of animals is worth studying? How would a community benefit from having leaders trained to promote the humane treatment of animals?

Learning & Innovation Skills

The Cape Wildlife Center is dedicated to the care and healing of sick, injured, or orphaned wildlife. Located on Cape Cod, Massachusetts, the center teaches vets and other students how to handle and care for animals such as raccoons, skunks, squirrels, rabbits, and a variety of wild birds. The program teaches students how to make quick decisions and solve problems that affect the animals they work with. Students in the program may raise an orphaned opossum or help rehabilitate a wounded eagle. How would someone interested in becoming a veterinarian benefit from this program?

pet food companies or care for animals used in medical research. Researchers might also work in special study areas to discover better ways to treat certain conditions. These veterinary specialties are similar to medical specialties for humans. They include radiology (taking X-rays), cancer studies, cardiac (heart) studies, and ophthalmology (eye care). These veterinarians are required to take four additional years of training in their area of specialty.

Vets are part of the overall community. They use their skills to help animals in the towns and cities where they live. Many vets participate in animal rescue projects. These projects are designed to

Veterinarians will treat this sick sea lion before releasing it back into the wild.

save wild animals that are found wounded or sick. These projects may also rescue pets that are abandoned, injured, or lost in disasters.

Animals—both in homes and in the wild—need human help. Helping animals begins by taking good care of your own pets. Just as a human being needs a doctor and regular medical checkups, so do household pets. Vets recommend medicines, diet habits, and ways to better care for animals.

Beyond the home, you can work with vets in wild animal rescue programs. You can volunteer in nature preserves or humane shelters. These volunteer experiences give you an inside look at a career in veterinary medicine. Anyone interested in becoming a vet needs to work hard. They also need to have a love and appreciation for animals.

Some Famous Veterinarians

Marty Becker (?–) may be one of the best-known vets in North America. He believes in a special relationship between pets and people that he calls The Bond. He is regularly seen on ABC-TV's *Good Morning America*. He also appears on Animal Planet and writes a newspaper column called "Pet Connection."

Nicholas Dodman (1946–) is a veterinarian and director of the Animal Behavior Clinic at the Cumming School of Veterinary Medicine, Tufts University. An author of many books about raising and caring for cats and dogs, he is probably best known for his book *Dogs Behaving Badly.*

W. Jean Dodds (1941–) started Hemopet, a nonprofit animal blood bank. She is a well-known veterinarian who specializes in research on vaccines. A graduate of the Ontario Veterinary College in Toronto, she has won many awards for her research into animal blood diseases.

Lucy Spelman (1963–) is a dedicated researcher who hopes to preserve endangered species through her work. Her patients include endangered animals from around the globe. She works with giant pandas in China, Asian elephants in Burma, giant river otters in Guyana, and mountain gorillas in Rwanda. She is a former director of the Smithsonian Institution's National Zoo.

James Alfred Wight (1916–1995) began working as a veterinarian in 1940. He is better known to many as James Herriot, the author of many autobiographical books about working as a veterinarian.

GLOSSARY

anatomy (uh-NAT-uh-mee) study of the physical structure of a body, including muscles, bones, and organs

anesthesia (an-iss-THEE-szuh) medicine that makes a patient insensitive to pain

antibiotics (an-ti-bye-OT-iks) medicine that kills infection caused by bacteria

contagious (kuhn-TAY-juhss) able to be spread by direct contact with something or someone already carrying a disease

diagnose (dye-uhg-NOHS) to identify an illness or medical condition

domesticating (duh-MESS-tuh-kay-ting) taming

sedated (si-DAY-ted) put to sleep with medicine

snare (SNAIR) a type of animal trap

tranquilizer (TRANGK-wuhl-ize-ur) a medicine that calms a patient

vaccines (vak-SEENZ) medicine that prevents a patient from contracting a disease

veterinary (VET-ur-uh-ner-ee) dealing with the diseases or medical conditions of animals

For More Information

Books

Ferguson's Careers in Focus: Animal Care. New York:
Ferguson Publishing Company, 2006.

Herriot, James. *James Herriot's Dog Stories: Warm and Wonderful Stories about
the Animals Herriot Loves Best.* New York: St. Martin's Griffin, 2006.

Jackson, Donna M. *ER Vets: Life in an Animal Emergency
Room.* Boston: Houghton Mifflin, 2005.

Web Sites

The Humane Society of the United States
www.hsus.org/pets/pet_care/choosing_a_veterinarian.html
Learn about the Humane Society and get information
about choosing a vet for your pets

Talk to the Vet
www.talktothevet.com
Ask questions about being a vet and get answers from real veterinarians

INDEX

ABOUT THE AUTHOR

Barbara A. Somervill writes children's nonfiction books on
a variety of topics. As a writer, she has had many different
cool careers—teacher, news reporter, author, scriptwriter,
and restaurant critic. She believes that researching new and
different topics makes writing every book an adventure.
When she is not writing, Ms. Somervill plays duplicate
bridge, reads avidly, and travels.